SKILL BUILDER
MATHS

LEVEL
2

PUFFIN BOOKS

An imprint of Penguin Random House

PUFFIN BOOKS

USA | Canada | UK | Ireland | Australia
New Zealand | India | South Africa | China | Singapore

Puffin Books is part of the Penguin Random House group of companies
whose addresses can be found at global.penguinrandomhouse.com

Published by Penguin Random House India Pvt. Ltd
4th Floor, Capital Tower 1, MG Road,
Gurugram 122 002, Haryana, India

First published in Puffin Books by Penguin Random House India 2018

Text, design and illustrations copyright © Quadrum Solutions Pvt. Ltd 2018
Series copyright © Penguin Random House India 2018

ISBN 9780143445166

Design and layout by Quadrum Solutions Pvt. Ltd
Printed at Repro India Limited

www.penguin.co.in

Dear Moms and Dads,

There's no better way to prepare your children for their future than to equip them with all the skills they need to grow into confident adults. The Skill Builder series has been created to hone subject skills as well as twenty-first century skills so that children develop not just academic skills but also life skills.

The books in the Skill Builder series focus on numerical, science and English language skills. Recognizing that children learn best while having fun, the books in this series have been created with a high 'fun' quotient. Each subject is dealt with across four levels, so you can choose the level that best suits your child's learning stage.

The Skill Builder: Maths books have been created by academic experts who have devised a special skill development chart to help you track the skills your child acquires as they complete the activities.

It has been great creating this series with my highly charged Quadrum team—our academic experts, Krupa Shah and Naimisha Sanghavi, who spent hours crafting each page; Esha, who designed every page to be a visual treat; Kushal, who painstakingly laid out every number and sign; Bishnupriya and Ruby, who read and re-read every word; and Kunjli, who was the conscience of the entire series. And of course, the Puffin team— Sohini and Ashwitha—who added value at every step. When you have a great team, you're bound to have a great book.

I do hope you and your child enjoy the series as much as we have enjoyed creating it.

Sonia Mehta

PS: We'd love your feedback, so do write in to us at

funlearningbooks@quadrumltd.com

SMART SKILL BUILDER CHART

Here is a snapshot of the skills your child will acquire as they complete the activities.

- **Number and computing skills:** Basic arithmetic skills including addition, subtraction, multiplication and division.
- **Data Representation skills:** The ability to structure and present data in a meaningful way.
- **Spatial skills:** The ability to visualize in 3D and develop an intuitive feel for shape and space. Also involves the concepts of traditional geometry.
- **Measurement skills:** A practical understanding of critical measurements and estimation concepts, including length, height, quantity, weight, distance and time.
- **Logical reasoning skills:** The ability to use a rational, systematic series of steps to come to a conclusion.
- **Patterning skills:** The ability to identify patterns and make logical connections between sequences, sizes, shapes and numbers.
- **Creative thinking skills:** The ability to view a problem creatively from different angles.
- **Critical thinking/problem solving skills:** Rationalizing, analysing, evaluating, and interpreting information to make informed judgments.

Page No.	Activity	Number and Computing	Data Presentation	Spatial Sense	Measurement	Logical Reasoning	Patterning	Creative Thinking	Critical Thinking
4	STEPPING STONES	☺					☺		
5	NUMBER NAME FUN	☺	☺						
6	BUBBLE NUMBERS	☺				☺			
7	EVEN COUNTING	☺	☺				☺		
8	EQUAL OR NOT?		☺	☺					
9	ODD COUNTING	☺					☺		
10	CAR RACING	☺					☺		
11	TENS TRAINS	☺	☺			☺	☺		
12	TASTY TANGY TWIST			☺	☺			☺	
14	SKIPPING IS FUN	☺	☺				☺		☺
16	ADD AND COLOUR	☺	☺			☺			
17	SHOPPING SPREE	☺	☺						☺
18	READING FUN	☺	☺						☺
19	HELLO JUGGLER	☺	☺						☺

Page	Activity
20	BUILDING BLOCKS
21	STACK THEM UP
22	HOW MANY PARTS?
23	PAUL'S DAY
24	PARKING CARS
26	TO THE MINUTE
27	COLOURFUL CLOCKS
28	SAM GOES SHOPPING
29	CHANGE MAKER
30	KEN'S KENNEL
31	ORANGE JUICE
32	CAKES
34	FRUIT FUN
35	MATCH THEM
36	ADDITION SQUARES
37	ADDITION PYRAMID
38	DART BOARD
39	PIZZA PIECES
40	MY SCHEDULE
42	TINA'S TIME
44	FIND AND MEASURE
45	JUICE BAR
46	SHAPES AROUND US
48	FLOWER POWER
49	FUN WITH MARBLES
50	CUPCAKE MANIA
51	COLOURFUL PINWHEEL
52	MONTHLY MANIA
53	JOVIAL JULY
54	PARTY TIME
56	CODE BREAKER
57	COOKIE CRUNCH
58	3, 2, 1 LIFT OFF
59	SET THE TIME

STEPPING STONES

Fill in the missing numbers on the blank stepping stones.
Some numbers have been filled in for you.

193

197

190

199

START

FINISH

187

NUMBER NAME FUN

Write the number names for the numbers in the balloons.

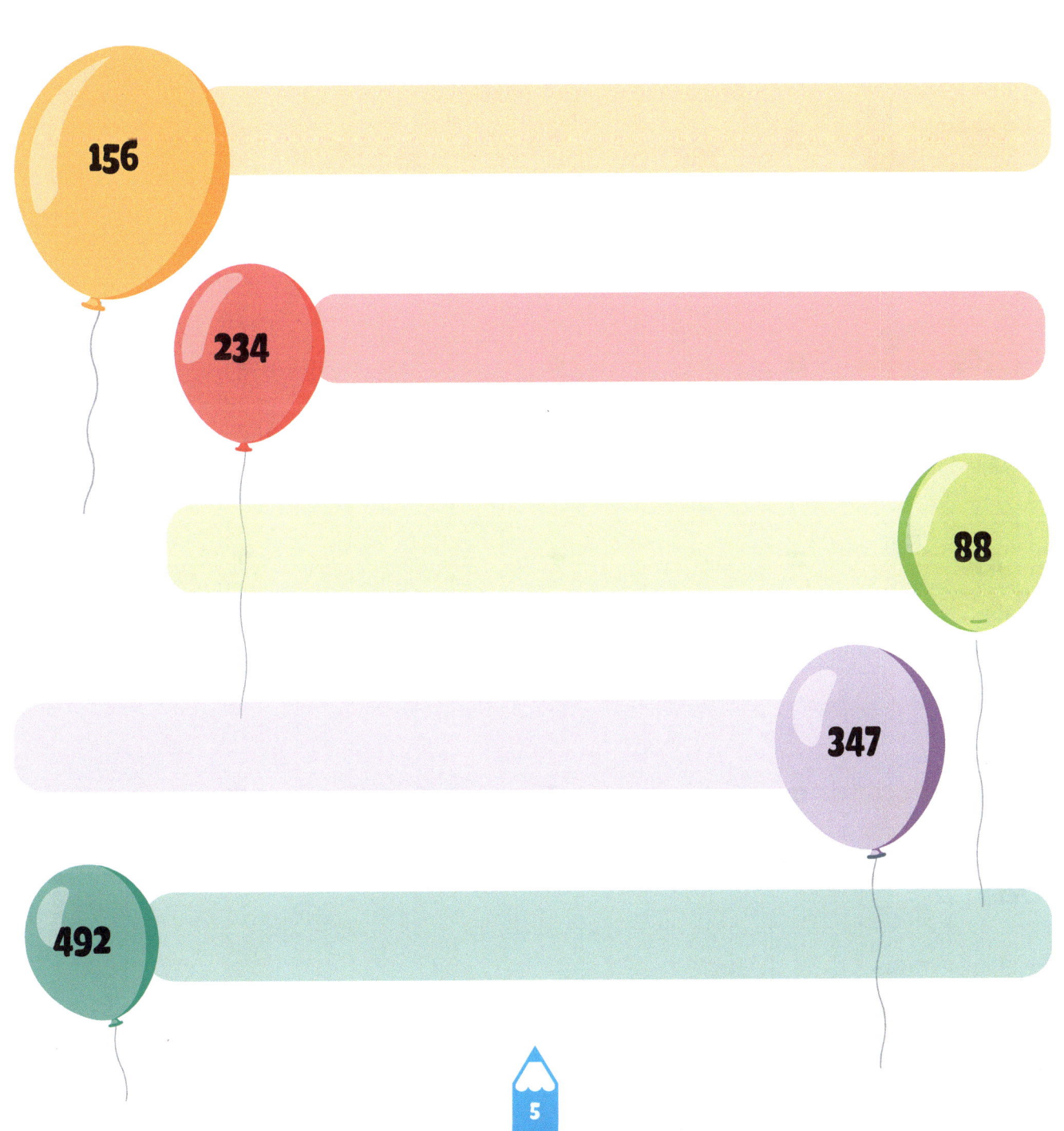

BUBBLE NUMBERS

Susie likes to expand everything! Help her by writing the numbers below in expanded form. One has been done for you.

237 = 200 + 30 + 7

765 = ___ + ___ + ___

430 = ___ + ___ + ___

291 = ___ + ___ + ___

548 = ___ + ___ + ___

EVEN COUNTING

Now Susie is filling in the rings with even numbers from 20 to 40. Can you help out?

EQUAL OR NOT

Some kids have cut up pieces of paper in different shapes.
Colour the pieces that have been cut into equal parts.

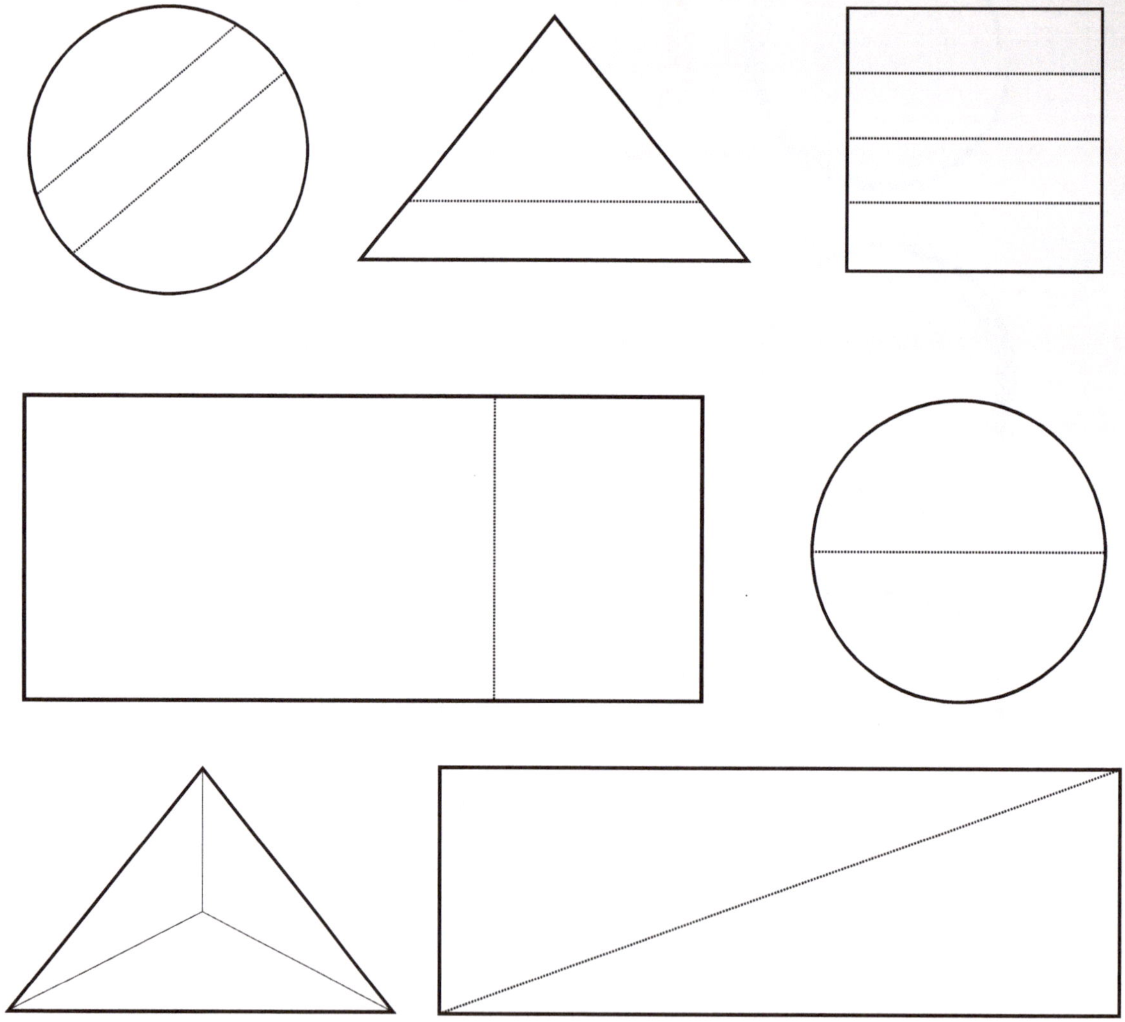

ODD COUNTING

Fill in the yellow circles with odd numbers from 35 to 55.

35

Start →

55

CAR RACING

The race is about to begin. The cars are numbered and have to be arranged in ascending order. Can you write the correct order in the boxes?

167

216

87

78

176

TENS TRAIN

These trains are ready to chug off. Look at the number on each engine. Add 10 to it and write the answer in the first coach. Continue the sequence for the rest of the coaches.

23

41

36

17

TASTY TANGY TWIST

Here is a fun and simple recipe to give fruits a tasty, tangy twist. Ask a grown-up to chop the fruits for you.

Ingredients:

Apple—1 cup

Orange—1 cup

Banana—½ cup

Pineapple—½ cup

Grapes—½ cup

Pomegranate—¼ cup

Lemon juice—1 teaspoon

Chaat masala—1 teaspoon

Sugar—½ teaspoon

Salt—¼ teaspoon

Pepper—¼ teaspoon

Method:

- Peel and chop the fruits.
- In a big bowl, mix the chopped fruits well.
- Add the lemon juice, chaat masala, sugar, salt and pepper to the bowl.
- Mix it all up and enjoy!

Take a picture of your fruit chaat and paste it in the space below.

Ask your family and friends to taste your dish and write down their comments below.

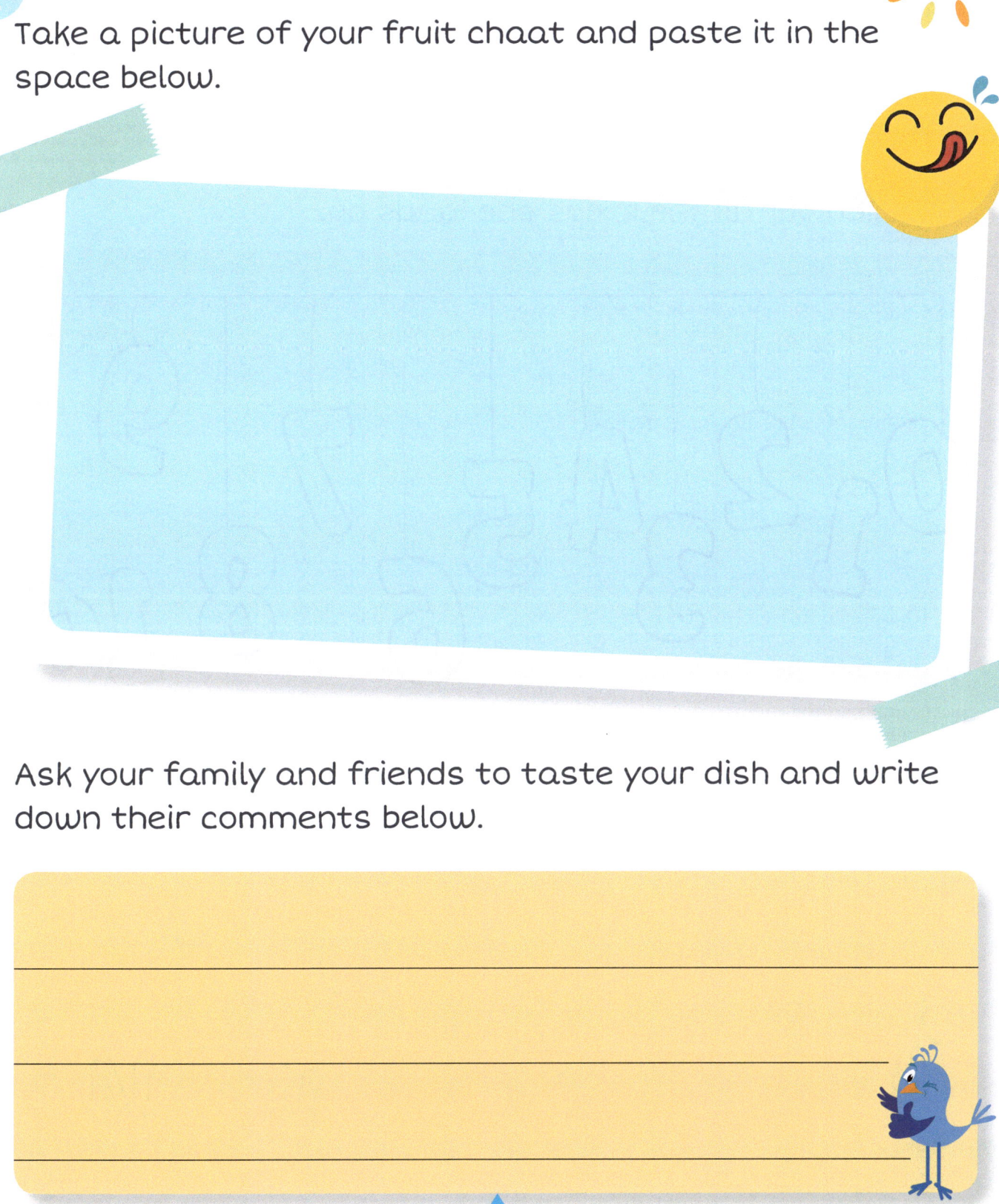

SKIPPING IS FUN

Tia likes to skip steps. Today she is skipping every two steps. Colour all the steps she lands on.

Now, Tia is skipping every three steps. Colour all the steps she lands on.

11 12 13 14 15 16 17 18 19 20

16 17 18 19 20 21 22 23 24 25 26 27 28 29 30

ADD AND COLOUR

Solve the following sums. Colour the answer box red if the answer is an odd number and blue if the answer is an even number.

$$37 + 51 = $$

$$64 + 32 = $$

$$22 + 52 = $$

$$73 + 26 = $$

$$48 + 20 = $$

$$41 + 54 = $$

SHOPPING SPREE

Four friends went out for dessert. They each chose two of their favourite desserts. Can you help calculate how much each of them has to pay?

cost 30

cost 32

cost 27

cost 23

cost 35

Ben

_____ + _____

Jojo

_____ + _____

Rita

_____ + _____

Mike

_____ + _____

READING FUN

Each student was given 20 books to read. They are holding up signs that indicate the number of books they have read. Subtract the numbers using the number line to find the number of books they have left to read.

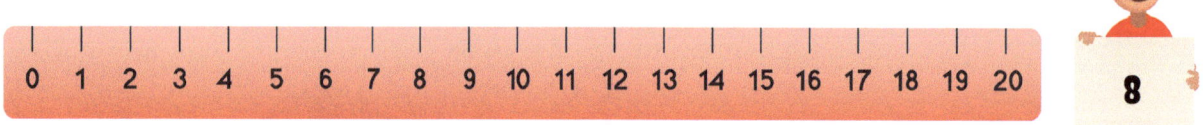

8

Unread books

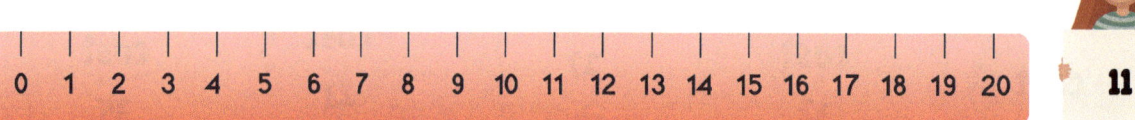

11

Unread books

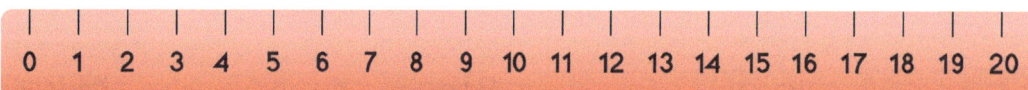

15

Unread books

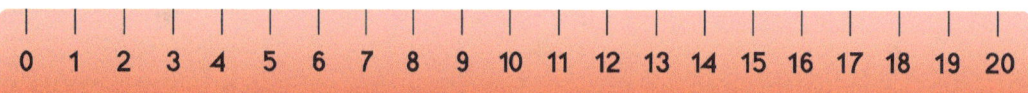

7

Unread books

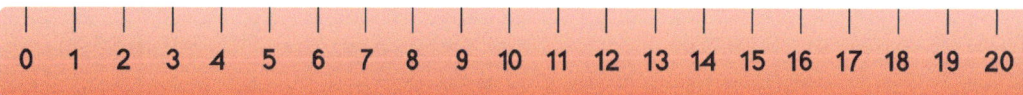

12

Unread books

HELLO JUGGLER

Subtract the numbers in each ball and colour them according to code below.

5—red **35**—green **11**—blue **46**—purple **24**—orange **43**—yellow

77
− 31
___

67
− 24
___

48
− 24
___

55
− 20
___

58
− 53
___

47
− 36
___

BUILDING BLOCKS

Identify the number pattern and fill in the blocks.

Row 1: 22, 25, 28, __, __, __, __, __

Row 2: 170, 177, 184, __, __, __, __, __

Row 3: 68, 78, 88, __, __, __, __, __

Row 4: 123, 128, 133, __, __, __, __, __

Row 5: 293, 295, 297, __, __, __, __

STACK THEM UP

Tim loves to play with his stacking rings. Colour this picture according to the instructions.

Colour the third ring red.

Colour the eighth ring yellow.

Colour the tenth ring light blue.

Colour the first ring green.

Colour the fourth ring pink.

Colour the seventh ring purple.

Colour the sixth ring orange.

Colour the second ring brown.

Colour the ninth ring black.

Colour the fifth ring dark blue.

HOW MANY PARTS

Here are some cakes of different shapes. Help the baker count and write the number of equal parts in each.

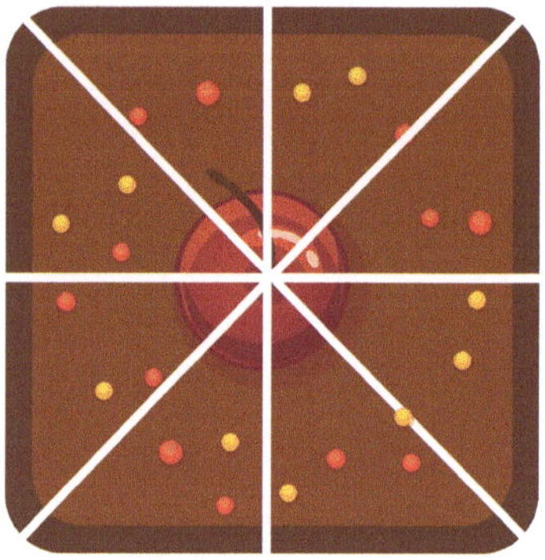

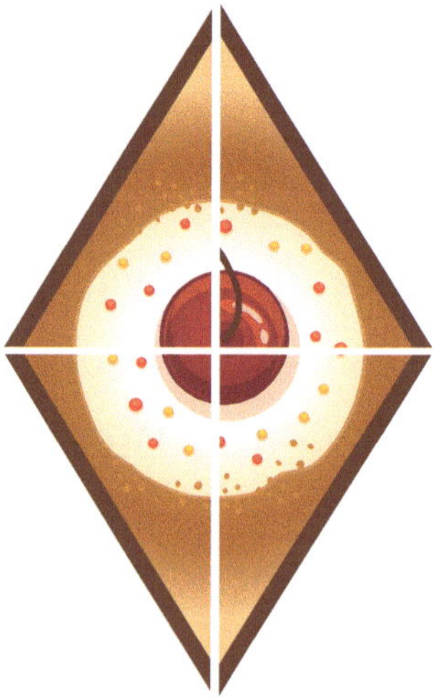

PAUL'S DAY

Paul has a very busy day. Look at the clocks and write down the time on each to help him stay on schedule.

It's time for Paul to wake up.

It is time to go to school.

Break time!

Lunch time.

Dinner time.

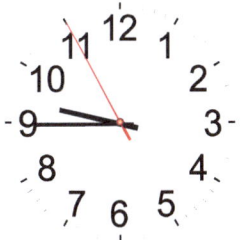

Time to go to bed.

PARKING CARS

There are some cars in this parking lot. Answer the questions below.

How many cars are there?

How many wheels does each car have?

How many wheels are there in total in the parking lot?

Some time later, 3 more cars and 5 bikes are parked here. Now answer the questions below.

How many cars are there now?

How many car wheels in total are in the parking lot?

How many bikes are there?

How many bike wheels are there in total?

How many wheels are there in total?

TO THE MINUTE

Penny is learning to tell the time. She can't remember the numbers on the clock and how many minutes they stand for. Can you help her out by filling in the missing numbers?

5

11

1

45

7

20

COLOURFUL CLOCKS

Help Tina match the time in the boxes to the clocks. Then colour the clocks in the same colour as the boxes.

5:15

7:45

9:15

2:30

11:00

12:45

SAM GOES SHOPPING

Sam is making a shopping list. The first column shows you what he wants to buy and how much it costs. The second column shows you how much money he has. Colour the object if Sam has the money to buy it and cross it out if he doesn't.

Teddy bear

120

10 10 10 10 20 20

Book

25

20 10

Toy truck

135

50 50

Ball

220

50 50 50 50 20

Paints

43

20 10 10 2 2 2

CHANGE MAKER

Sally and her friends buy some fruits. They need your help to calculate how much change they should each get from the shopkeeper.

Ron bought for

120

Ron gave

200

How much should Ron get back?

Sally bought for

230

Sally gave

500

How much should Sally get back?

Tim bought for

45

Tim gave

100

How much should Tim get back?

Bob bought for

85

Bob gave

200

How much should Bob get back?

Tia bought for

112

Tia gave

150

How much should Tia get back?

KEN'S KENNEL

Help Rita build a kennel for her dog Ken. Measure the lines below and write down the lengths in centimetres in the space given.

A _____

B _____

C _____

D _____

E _____

F _____

G _____

H _____

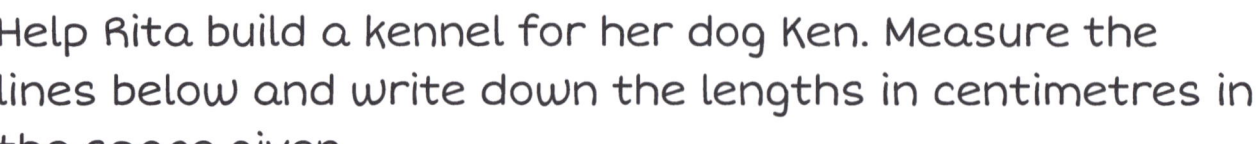

ORANGE JUICE

Amanda has 35 oranges. She needs 3 oranges to make one glass of orange juice.

How many glasses of orange juice can she make?

Are there any extra oranges? If yes, how many?

CAKES

Ben the baker has an order for 8 cakes. He has to cut chocolate cakes into halves, butterscotch cakes into thirds and strawberry cakes into quarters. Colour the halves in brown, thirds in yellow and quarters in pink.

How many groups can you make?

There are 8 apples. How many groups of 2 can you make?

There are 9 pears. How many groups of 3 can you make?

 There are 10 bananas. How many groups of 5 can you make?

There are 8 pineapples. How many groups of 4 can you make?

MATCH THEM

Match the 2D shapes in the centre row to their corresponding 3D shapes in the top and the bottom rows.

ADDITION SQUARES

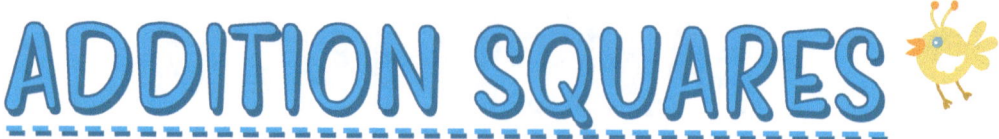

Add these numbers vertically and horizontally and write down the answers in the blank spaces.

34	57	
61	92	

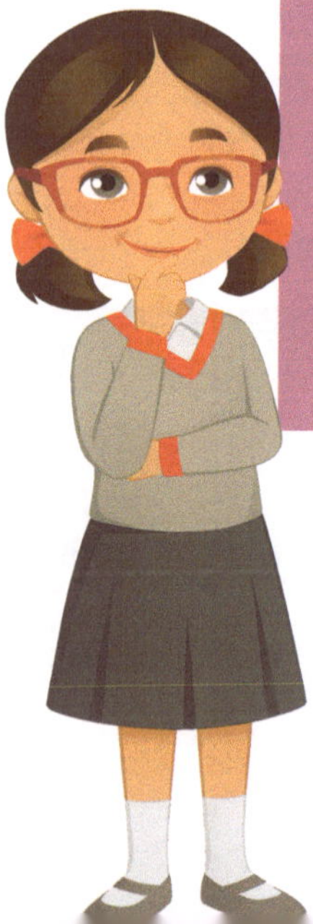

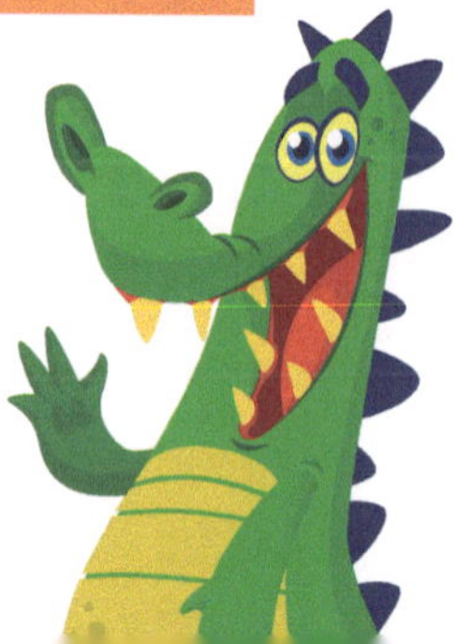

ADDITION PYRAMID

To reach the top of the pyramid, you must write down the correct answers in each box. To find the answers, just remember that the bottom two blocks add up to the number in the top block. One has been done for you.

78
51 39
19
11 10
8 6 6
7 1 4 6

DART BOARD

Some kids have painted these dart boards in different ways. Look at each board and circle the fraction that represents the coloured area.

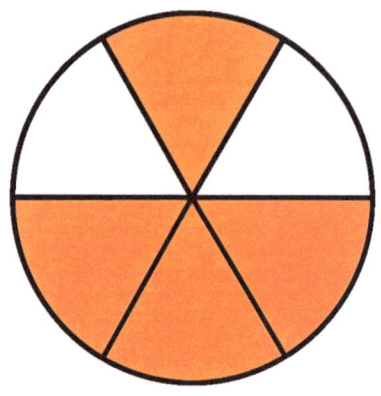

$\frac{2}{4}$ $\frac{4}{6}$ $\frac{2}{6}$

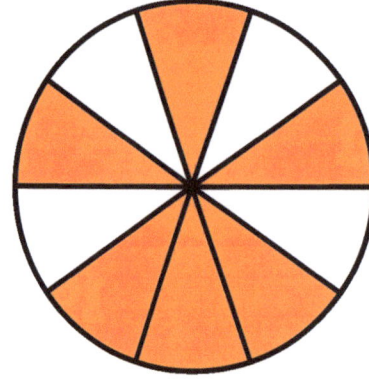

$\frac{6}{10}$ $\frac{4}{5}$ $\frac{5}{10}$

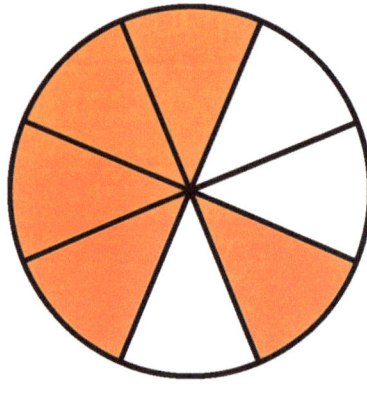

$\frac{4}{8}$ $\frac{2}{4}$ $\frac{5}{8}$

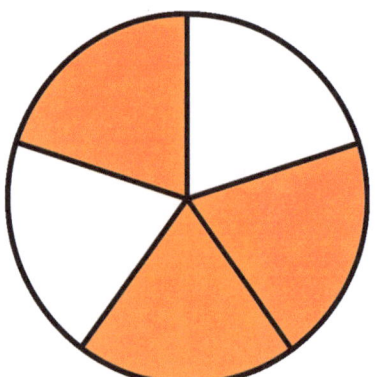

$\frac{2}{5}$ $\frac{3}{5}$ $\frac{5}{7}$

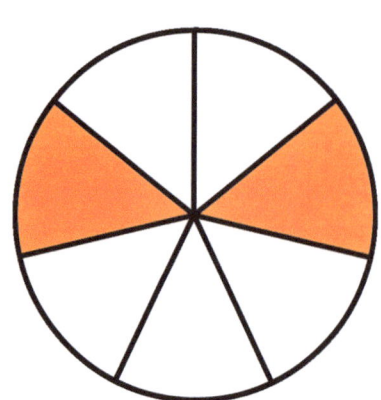

$\frac{3}{7}$ $\frac{2}{6}$ $\frac{2}{7}$

38

PIZZA PIECES

Can you help Sia cut these pizzas into equal parts according to the instructions below each one? Then write down the fraction that one piece of each pizza makes.

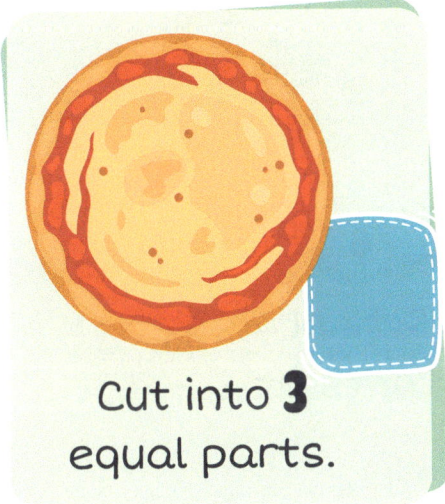

Cut into **3** equal parts.

Cut into **4** equal parts.

Cut into **6** equal parts.

Cut into **5** equal parts.

Cut into **2** equal parts.

Cut into **8**. equal parts.

MY SCHEDULE

Write the time of the day at which you do these activities. Then mark the time on the clock faces by drawing the hands of the clocks.

I wake up at

School
starts at

I can
play at

I get home from
school at

I eat
lunch at

My mom/dad comes home
from work at

.

I go to bed at

.

I eat dinner at

.

TINA'S TIME

Can you help Tina mark these dates on her calendar?

- Tina doesn't have school on the 5th. Cross it out.

- Tina's birthday is on the 20th. Can you decorate the date for her?

- How many days are left in the month after Tina's birthday? _____

- Tina has a dentist's appointment on the 12th. Circle it so that she doesn't forget.

- Draw a square around the last Monday of the month.

- How many weekdays are there in the month? _____

November

Sun	Mon	Tues	Wed	Thurs	Fri	Sat
					1	2
3	4	5	6	7	8	9
10	11	12	13	14	15	16
17	18	19	20	21	22	23
24	25	26	27	28	29	30

FIND AND MEASURE

Look for the following things around the house. Then measure them from tip to tip using a ruler. Write down the measurements in the boxes. You may also draw the objects.

pencil

cm

hand towel

cm

school bag

cm

shoe sole

cm

serving spoon

cm

eraser

cm

JUICE BAR

Mary is making some delicious drinks for her friends. Add the ingredients to find the total volume of each glass of juice.

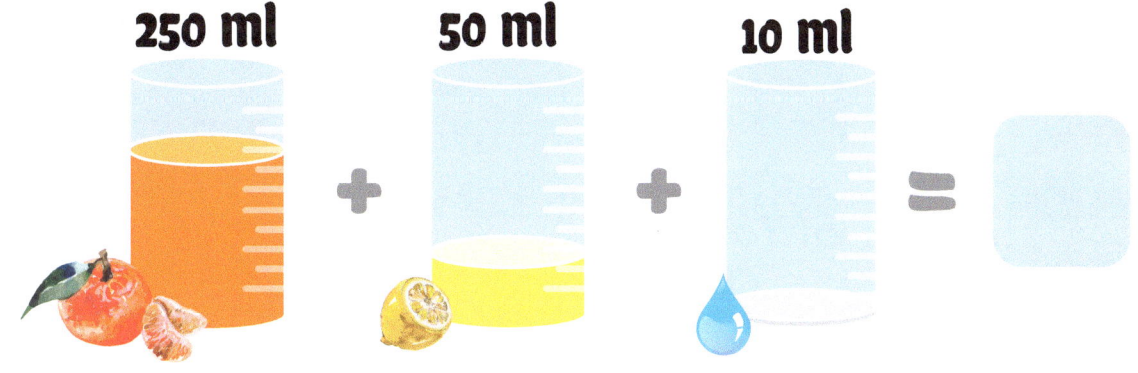

250 ml + **50 ml** + **10 ml** =

300 ml + **120 ml** =

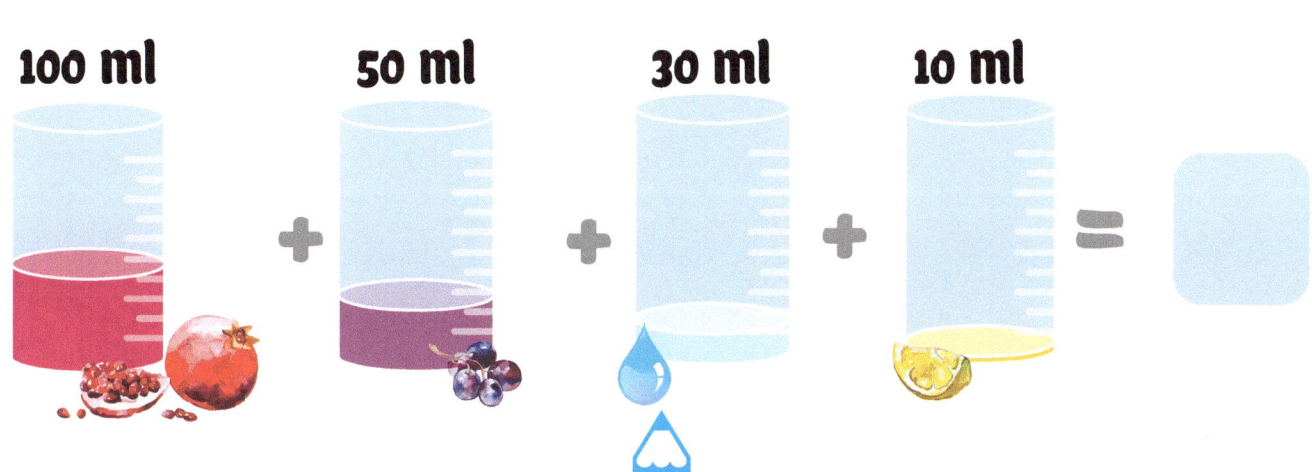

100 ml + **50 ml** + **30 ml** + **10 ml** =

SHAPES AROUND US

Here are some 3D shapes. Can you spot any objects with these shapes around you? Write down how many faces each 3D shape has and draw three or four objects that have the same shape.

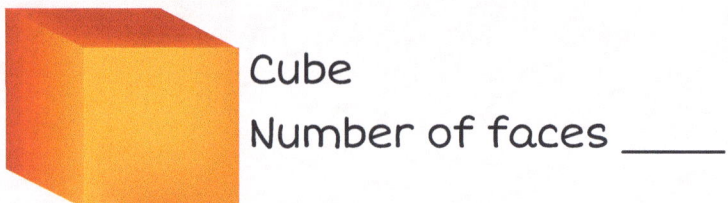

Cube

Number of faces _____

Sphere

Number of faces _____

Cylinder

Number of faces _____

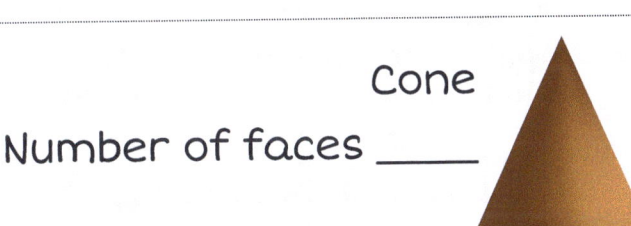

Cone

Number of faces _____

Cuboid

Number of faces _____

FLOWER POWER

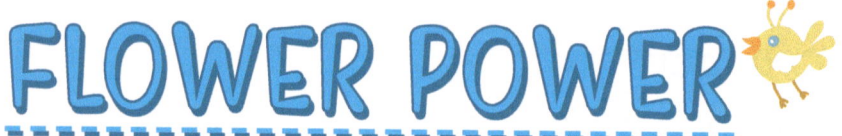

Joe has used tally marks to count the number of flowers in his garden. Can you colour the graph to show how many of each type he has?

Rose	Lily	Tulip	Daffodil	Iris	Carnation
𝍸	𝍸 𝍸 𝍷𝍷𝍷	𝍸 𝍷𝍷	𝍸 𝍸	𝍸 𝍸 𝍷	𝍷𝍷𝍷

13						
12						
11						
10						
9						
8						
7						
6						
5						
4						
3						
2						
1						
	Rose	Lily	Tulip	Daffodil	Iris	Carnation

FUN WITH MARBLES

Here are some marbles in a bag. Can you answer the questions below? Remember, your answers must be in the form of fractions!

What is the total number of marbles in the bag?

What fraction of the total is made up by yellow marbles?

What fraction of the total is made up by red marbles?

What fraction of the total is made up by blue or green marbles?

What fraction of the total is not made up by pink marbles?

CUPCAKE MANIA

Ben has baked some delicious cupcakes. He's arranged them in the groups below to put them into boxes.

What fraction of the box do the chocolate cupcakes make?

What fraction of the box do the strawberry cupcakes make?

What fraction of the box do the butterscotch cupcakes make?

What fraction of the box do the blueberry cupcakes make?

What fraction of the box do the kiwi cupcakes make?

What fraction of the box do the chocolate cupcakes make?

COLOURFUL PINWHEEL

This pinwheel was once colourful but all the colour has been washed away. Colour this pinwheel according to the information given and answer the questions that follow.

- 4 green sections

- 2 blue sections

- 2 yellow sections

- 1 section each in red and orange

What fraction do the red sections make?

What fraction do the yellow sections make?

What fraction do the blue sections make?

What fraction do the green sections make?

MONTHLY MANIA

Read the clues below and write down the correct name of the month in the space given.

I'm the month before December.	_____
I'm the ninth month of the year.	_____
I'm the month after July.	_____
I'm the only month with 28 or 29 days in it.	_____
I'm the third month of the year.	_____
I'm the month after April.	_____
I'm the seventh month of the year.	_____
I'm the last month of the year.	_____
I'm the month after September.	_____
I'm the month after May.	_____
I'm the fourth month of the year.	_____
I'm the first month of the year	_____

JOVIAL JULY

Jack can't wait for July. He has some things marked on his calendar. Take a look at it and answer the questions that follow.

JULY 2019

Sun	Mon	Tues	Wed	Thurs	Fri	Sat
	1	2	3	4	5	6
7	8	9	10	11	12	13
14	15	16	17	18	19	20
21	22	23	24	25	26	27
28	29	30	31			

How many Mondays are there in July? _____

What date is the painting competition on? _____

What day on the calendar is the 3rd? _____

What are the day and date of Jack's birthday? _____

Does Pizza Day fall on a weekday or weekend? _____

PARTY TIME

It's Ron's birthday and the house is full of balloons. Can you count the balloons using tally marks?

Balloons	Tally	Numbers
blue		
green		
yellow		
purple		
red		

How many balloons in total were used at Ron's birthday party?

Which colour was used the least at the party?

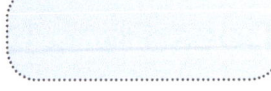

3 balloons in each colour were added. Fill the table again according to the new numbers

Balloons	Tally	Numbers
blue		
green		
yellow		
purple		
red		

What was the total number of balloons at Ron's birthday party?

CODE BREAKER

Katy has to break the code to find the clues to some hidden treasure. Help her by writing the numbers that match the Roman numerals below.

IX
_____

VIII
_____

XXIV
_____

XXXVI
_____

XXIX
_____

XXXVII
_____

IV
_____

XXXI
_____

CRUNCHY COOKIES

Ruby is baking cookies in batches. Help her calculate the number of cookies she has baked in each batch. Write the multiplication statement and answer for each.

☐ × ☐ = ☐

☐ × ☐ = ☐

☐ × ☐ = ☐

☐ × ☐ = ☐

3, 2, 1 LIFT OFF

Solve the multiplication sums on the astronaut suits. Then colour the level of the rocket and the astronaut suit it matches using the same colour. Fire away!

Rockets: 5, 8, 0, 18, 63

Astronaut suits:
- 3 × 6
- 7 × 9
- 4 × 2
- 5 × 1
- 8 × 0

SET THE TIME

Mike's watch stopped working a couple of times during the day. Can you help him set it to the right time by marking the correct time on the faces below?

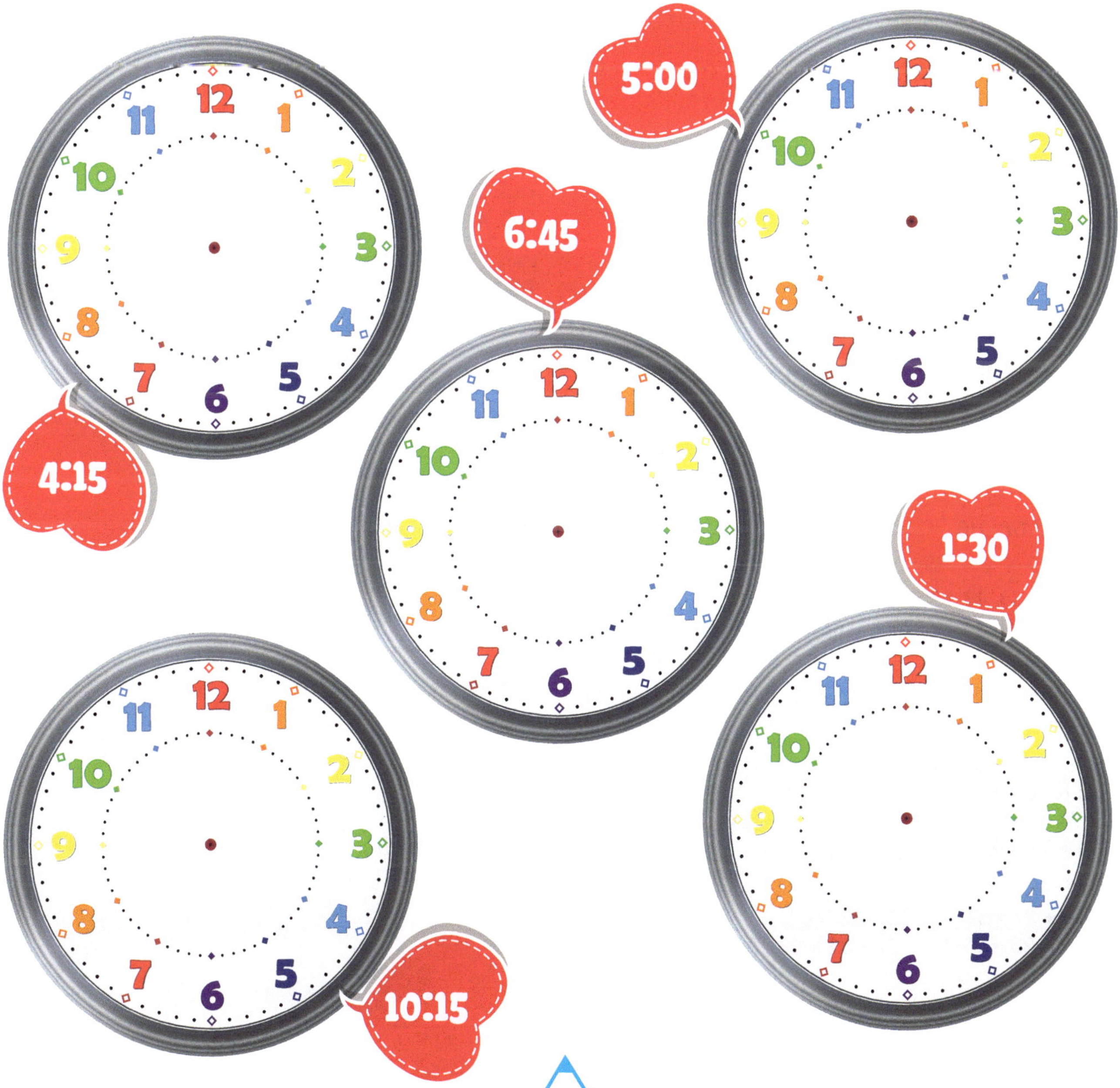

5:00

6:45

4:15

1:30

10:15

ANSWERS

page 4 STEPPING STONES
184, 185, 186, 187, 188, 189, 190, 191, 192, 193, 194, 195, 196, 197, 198, 199, 200, 201, 202, 203

page 5 NUMBER NAME FUN
156—One hundred and fifty-six; 234—Two hundred and thirty-four; 88—Eighty-eight; 347—Three hundred and forty-seven; 492—Four hundred and ninety-two

page 6 BUBBLE NUMBERS
700+60+5; 400+30+0; 200+90+1; 500+40+8

page 7 EVEN COUNTING
20, 22, 24, 26, 28, 30, 32, 34, 36, 38, 40

page 8 EQUAL OR NOT

page 9 ODD COUNTING
35, 37, 39, 41, 43, 45, 47, 49, 51, 53, 55

page 10 CAR RACING
78, 87, 167, 176, 216

page 11 TENS TRAINS
Train 1—23, 33, 43, 53, 63, 73; Train 2—41, 51, 61, 71, 81, 91; Train 3—36, 46, 56, 66, 76, 86; Train 4—17, 27, 37, 47, 57, 67

page 14–15 SKIPPING IS FUN
These numbers will be coloured: 2, 4, 6, 8, 10, 12, 14, 16, 18, 20
These numbers will be coloured: 3, 6, 9, 12, 15, 18, 21, 24, 27, 30

page 16 ADD AND COLOUR
Boxes to be coloured blue: 37 + 51 = 88, 64 + 32 = 96, 22 + 52 = 74, 48 + 20 = 68; Boxes to be coloured red: 73 + 26 = 99, 41 + 54 = 95

page 17 SHOPPING SPREE
Ben: 30 + 27 = 57; Jojo: 35 + 23 = 58; Rita: 32 + 23 = 55; Mike: 27 + 32 = 59

page 18 READING FUN
20 - 8 = 12; 20 - 11 = 9; 20 - 15 = 5; 20 - 7 = 13; 20 - 12 = 8

page 19 HELLO JUGGLER
58 - 53 = 5 (red); 48 - 24 = 24 (orange); 77 - 31 = 46 (purple); 67 - 24 = 43 (yellow); 55 - 20 = 35 (green); 47 - 36 = 11 (blue)

page 20 BUILDING BLOCKS
1. 22, 25, 28... 31, 34, 37, 40, 43; 2. 68, 78, 88... 98, 3. 170, 177, 184... 191, 198, 205, 212, 219; 108, 118, 128, 138; 4. 123, 128, 133... 138, 143, 148, 153, 158; 5. 293, 295, 297... 299, 301, 303, 305, 307

page 21 STACK THEM UP

page 22 HOW MANY PARTS?
5; 8; 4; 4; 6

page 23 PAUL'S DAY
7:30 am; 9:15 am; 11:30 am; 12:45 pm; 6:30 pm; 9:45 pm

page 24–25 PARKING CARS
How many cars are there? 8
How many wheels does one car have? 4
How many wheels are there in total in the parking lot? 32
How many cars are there now? 11
How many car wheels are there? 44
How many bikes are there? 5
How many bike wheels are there? 10
How many wheels are there in total? 54

page 26 TO THE MINUTE

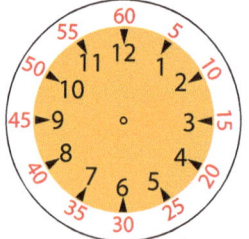

page 27 COLOURFUL CLOCKS

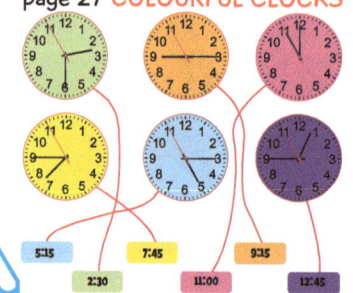

page 28 SAM GOES SHOPPING

Sam has the money to buy the book, the ball, and the paints. Sam does not have the money to buy the teddy bear and the toy truck.

page 29 CHANGE MAKER

Ron should get back 80. Sally should get back 270. Tim should get back 55. Bob should get back 115. Tia should get back 38.

page 30 KEN'S KENNEL

A—14.5 cm, B—6.2 cm, C—7.2 cm, D—10.9 cm, E—5.5 cm, F—8.6 cm, G—4.5 cm, H—2.5 cm

Note: Answers have been rounded off to the nearest decimal. Answers may vary slightly depending on the scale used.

Page 31 ORANGE JUICE

How many glasses of orange juice can she make? 11
Are there any extra oranges? If yes how many? 2

Page 32—33 CAKES

page 34 FRUIT FUN

4; 3; 2; 2

Page 35 MATCH THEM

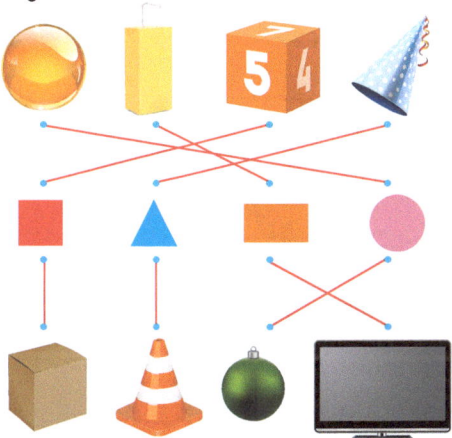

page 36 ADDITION SQUARES

34	57	91
61	92	153
95	149	244

page 37 ADDITION PYRAMID

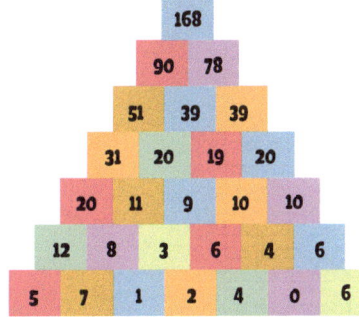

page 38 DART BOARD

Circled Answers: 4/6, 3/5, 6/10, 5/8, 2/7

page 39 PIZZA PIECES

page 40—41 MY SCHEDULE

Answers may vary.

page 42—43 TINA'S TIME

November						
Sun	Mon	Tues	Wed	Thurs	Fri	Sat
					1	2
3	4	5	6	7	8	9
10	11	12	13	14	15	16
17	18	19	20	21	22	23
24	25	26	27	28	29	30

How many days are left in the month after Tina's birthday? 10
How many weekdays are there in the month? 21

page 44 FIND AND MEASURE

Answers may vary.

page 45 JUICE BAR

310 ml, 420 ml, 190 ml

page 46—47 SHAPES AROUND US

cube—6 faces; sphere—1 face; cylinder—3 faces; cone—2 faces; cuboid—6 faces

page 48 FLOWER POWER

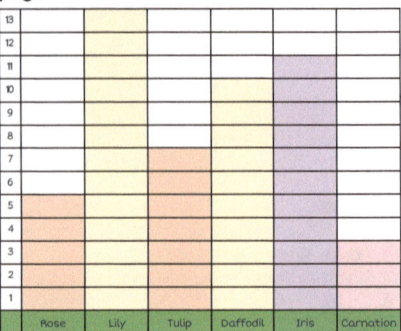

page 49 FUN WITH MARBLES

There are 19 marbles in the bag; What fraction of the total is made up by yellow marbles? 5/19; What fraction of the total is made up by red marbles? 0/19; What fraction of the total is made up by blue or green marbles? 11/19; What fraction of the tottal is not made up by pink marbles? 16/19

page 50 CUPCAKE MANIA
2/7, 5/7; 4/7, 3/7; 3/9, 6/9

page 51 COLOURFUL PINWHEEL

1/10; 2/10; 2/10; 4/10

page 52 MONTHLY MANIA
November; September; August; February; March; May; July; December; October; June; April; January

page 53 JOVIAL JULY
There are 5 Mondays; The painting competition is on July 15th, 2019; The 3rd is a Wednesday; Jack's birthday is on Thursday, July 11th 2019; It is on a Saturday, which is a weekend.

page 54—55 PARTY TIME

blue	ЖЖ II	7
green	ЖЖ I	6
yellow	IIII	4
purple	ЖЖ III	8
red	ЖЖ	5

30 balloons were used in total at Ron's birthday party.

Yellow was used least at the party.

blue	ЖЖ ЖЖ	10
green	ЖЖ IIII	9
yellow	ЖЖ II	7
purple	ЖЖ IIII	11
red	ЖЖ III	8

45 balloons were there at Ron's birthday party.

page 56 CODE BREAKER
IV-4; XXIX-29; XXIV-24; IX-9; VIII-8; XXXVI-36; XXXVII-37; XXXI-31

page 57 CRUNCHY COOKIES
5 x 5 = 25; 4 x 4 = 16; 3 x 6 = 18; 2 x 7 = 14

page 58 3, 2, 1 LIFT OFF

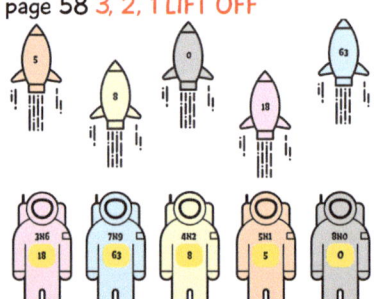

page 59 SET THE TIME

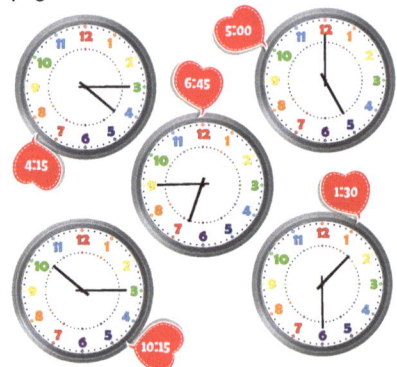